Iyabunmi A. Moore

If You Want It,
Speak It!

A Guidebook of Daily Affirmations for
Focus, Motivation and Success

PUBLISHED BY BLUE ARTISTS, LLC

This publication is designed to provide accurate and authoritative information in regard to the subject matter covered. It is sold with the understanding that the publisher is not engaged in rendering legal, accounting, or other professional service. If legal advice or other expert assistance is required, the services of a competent professional person should be sought.

INTRODUCTION

Life can be a challenge. The ups and downs, ins and outs, and frustrations and exhilarations can sometimes leave us feeling like we are on an amusement park ride. There are times when we are smiling in anticipation of something great happening only to within a short period of time be turning a corner just to be let down by an experience that leaves us screaming and wondering, "When is this going to be over?" Sometimes we feel so out of control and at other times we feel powerful enough to conquer the world. No matter how you are feeling at the moment always remember that this is a ride that YOU CHOOSE and you get to continue choosing your experience from this point forward. It can be the ride of your life or a ride from Hell. It's up to you.

The world is changing. It seems like the world's ON button is never shut off. Remember when TV would actually go off at night? I can still remember those red, green, blue, and black stripes, the stations' test patterns, before it would finally fade to black. On some stations, the national anthem would play to signal the closing of TV for that day before the all night static. As a society, we had the sense to know that there should be a time for quiet sleep. A time to unplug. It's amazing how the world has changed just in the last 30 years. TV NEVER shuts off. There are hundreds of channels as opposed to the 3 channels I grew up with. And as advances in technology increase, the number of negative messages that we are bombarded with daily from the world always being ON increases as well. We are bombarded with negativity from everywhere.

Unfortunately MOST of what we get from the outside world is negative. The news is always negative. From CNN...(I have a friend who says that CNN stands for constantly negative news) and the tabloids with its gossip and mayhem, to radio's explicit and sometimes violent lyrics, it's all negative. When you go out to restaurants and overhear conversations, it's usually people sharing negative things that are going on in their lives. Over and over and over we are repetitively taking in negativity. It can leave you shaking your head, feeling down, disillusioned, and pessimistic. And let's not forget the internet. We can't turn on the computer without some video or post of world calamity popping up in our faces. So many things are negative including people's bank accounts, and mindsets. More than any time in history, it's important that we disconnect from the negativity and have specific intent to reprogram ourselves with positivity to combat the negativity that seems to be on all sides. But the question is, "Just how do we do that?" I suggest cutting off the television for one thing. I call it the automatic income reducer. Also, turn off the radio. Turn your car into a university and as you drive listen to positive audio recordings instead. Here is another suggestion, and one of the most important things you can do, **learn to get into your own head.**

IT'S OKAY TO TALK TO YOURSELF

My sister/friend Tammy tells me that she has a cousin William who talks out loud to himself. Society calls William "off" and a little crazy but don't we all talk to ourselves at some point during the day? Okay maybe the fact that William does this constantly without any regard for who is around puts him in another category that we don't want to ever find ourselves in. But let's face it, sometimes when you are alone in your house, or riding along in your car, you just can't help saying what you are thinking out loud as if someone else were right there listening. I know I'm not the only one. You do it too, I'm sure. Some may call William crazy for talking to himself, but I am here to tell you that you are crazy if you DO NOT talk to yourself.

You need to start talking to yourself MORE EVERYDAY provided you are saying the **right** things to yourself, about yourself. This book will give you those right things to say. And once you have those right things to say, you need to start saying them over and over and over again. That's right. It's all about repetition. To truly REPROGRAM your mind repetition is key. I would suggest that you bombard your own mind using positive, productive, and uplifting thoughts with the same intensity that society works to feed you the opposite. In the morning when you rise, TALK TO YOURSELF. Wake up excited thinking great thoughts about how awesome your day is going to be, and verbalize those thoughts out loud. Throughout the day, TALK TO YOURSELF. Affirm great things to yourself about yourself all day long. At night before you fall asleep, when the subconscious is at it's most receptive state TALK TO YOURSELF. Repeat your positive affirmations over and over to yourself as you drift off to sleep. Do this for 45 days and it will probably become a habit. Man, what a life changing positive habit you would have developed. Did you know that every time you affirm something, whether out loud or in thought, you are placing your order for it? When you place your order, get ready to receive your request.

YOU PLACED THE ORDER

Have you ever had something show up EXACTLY when you needed it to? I'm sure we all have. I promise you that you are going to be thanking God that this book showed up for you at this place at this time in your life. It's not by luck or chance, but it is by LAW that you are reading this book right now. Don't know what I mean? Think about it. There is something that you have been hoping, wishing for, praying for, dreaming of, or thinking about that has caused this book to show up in your space. Can you put your finger on it? What thoughts have you been thinking that may have attracted this book to you? I do know this, if you follow the principles set forth here they are really going to bless you and be a great asset to you. Believe it or not, you ordered this book. With your mind you ordered this book. Whether you purchased this book yourself or were given it by a caring friend that loves you, you ordered it. We always get what we order. Whether we like the order or not, we get what we order. What we think about, we bring about.

You may already intentionally use affirmations to some extent, but using this book as a reference guide during your affirmation time will make it more effective. This book was born out of my own need to make my morning Hour of Power, the morning time that I use to connect to God and affirm my day and my life, even more fulfilling, enjoyable, and effective. It was spurred by the need for me to feed myself powerful words and phrases (without me having to think too hard and long) that keep me in harmony with all the good that I desire. It was brought into the physical by the need to agree OUT LOUD with the Universe on who I am, whose I am, what I have, and where I am. I know this well and you should too; what you put out, you live out. From here on out, be intentional about placing your order. Serve yourself up something delicious!

WORD POWER

I really don't think that people understand how much power the tongue has. The Bible tells us, "Life and death are in the power of the tongue," but people still don't truly believe this. If they did, they would take more care surrounding the words they speak. Words have incredible power. The spoken word is a creative force. In fact, sound is a major force in the act of creation and manifestation. Remember, God SPOKE and the world leapt into existence. I have seen this amazing word power displayed so actively in my life, helping me to manifest my goals and dreams. When you take heed to the same practices, so will you. There was a time when I felt a heavy weight on my shoulders. With 5 young kids, not enough income, a car that continuously broke down, no home of my own, and buried beneath mounds of debt, I just wanted to close my eyes and go to sleep forever. Have you ever felt that way? I am sure plenty of you can relate. You may feel like that now, or maybe you have felt that sometime in the past. How did I come up out of that you ask? Through doing the mental work of keeping my mind, thoughts, and words aligned with the good that I wanted for my family and myself. That mental work included using affirmations, vision boards, associating with like-minded individuals, keeping myself positive, and staying focused on my goals. Did it happen overnight? No! Did it happen? Yes! Was it easy? No. Was it worth it? You better believe it! I hope you are ready to pay the price to live your dreams. I hope you are ready to do the mental work that it takes to win. I hope you are ready to start using your words to create your world. As Rafiki declared about Simba stepping into his rightful place as king in *The Lion King*, "It is time!"

It is time for you to get further down the road to having, doing, and being all that you desire. With this book in your hand, you will feel sure about your journey. Within every cell of my being, I desire to see people be successful, WIN in life, and achieve their heart's desires. I know if you use this book, and its practices and applications as a practical tool in your life, help will always be present.

I was first introduced to affirmations as a 12- year-old middle school student (hint: get your kids involved in this great practice) when my father made me read *Think and Grow Rich*. To this day, he still has a copy of the report he made me write on Napoleon Hill's book. It wasn't until my adult years that I started using affirmations, although not consistently. In 2009, I started using them daily and consistently with phenomenal results in my life. As I incorporated affirmations into my prayer/meditation time and learned to put the feeling, emotion and visualization with the words, I began to draw out from within a new power that had been lying dormant inside of me that allowed that which I spoke to manifest with certainty.

The same will happen for you as you step into the practice of AFFIRMING YOUR LIFE DAILY with FEELING as the activator.

 USE THIS BOOK AS A TOOL

Sometimes we say affirmations and our mind may go blank, we don't know what to affirm next, or it may be a challenge to actually put words together in a well formed empowering way. In the following pages, you will find prewritten, inspiring, and exciting powerful words, phrases, and statements to invoke out loud to manifest into your reality. Keep this book with you at all times. Carry it in your purse, or keep it in your computer bag. Have several copies around the house so it's always accessible. When you are saying your affirmations, have it in your hand to help you pull out just the right affirming phrases that you need for that time. Call this book your "Affirmation Cheat Sheet", or "Guide Book."

These affirmations come directly from my personal journals. These affirmations are personal to me because I speak them all. Some I have created myself and some have come from my spiritual and millionaire mentors. I want you to pick out the ones that resonate with you. Allow these declarations to inspire you to create additional ones pertaining especially to what you are creating for your life. Space has been left in the back of each section for you to write your own Spirit-inspired affirmations. Remember, place your order. Proclaim EXACTLY what it is that you want.

As I explained earlier, repetition, feeling, and emotion are vitally important in the affirmation manifestation process. Don't worry if when you start to say your affirmations it feels difficult or like you are lying to yourself. That's normal for many people. Keep pushing through by repeating that phrase over and over. Get into the good feeling of already possessing that which you are speaking at the moment. For example, if when you affirm, "I am wealthy" you feel like you are lying to yourself because your mind keeps going to the $75 in your bank account, start by just thinking on the word "wealth" and PICTURE positively what YOU with wealth looks like. I bet that will put a smile on your face. If you are overweight and saying, "I am at my ideal weight makes you say, "Yeah right!" sarcastically. Repeat the word HEALTH think on it and picture what you in optimal health and a physically fit body would look like.

When you say your affirmations, repeat them over and over several times until you are emotionally involved in the words you are saying. I normally say each affirmation AT LEAST three times, putting energy and emotion into the words I am speaking. At the same time, I visualize what the manifestation of those words look like. Saying affirmations should leave you feeling exhilarated, energized, and expectant. So are you ready to get started? Let's go get what you came here for!

Here is one more note. The affirmations written in this book have been categorized into 4 sections; Money Affirmations, Health Affirmations, Success Affirmations, and Spiritual Connection Affirmations. In each section, I share a little of my journey in this given area and then I tell you some great things about yourself connected to that category, then it's your turn to do the talking. Let's roll!

MONEY AFFIRMATIONS

I am a money magnet. I like money and money likes me. In fact I will be bold and say that I love money. Money and I have a great relationship and it's getting better every day. What about you? How is your relationship with money? While I've always felt money was a great thing and always wanted lots of it, money and I have had our share of relationship struggles. My relationship with money has included overdrawn bank accounts, accumulating debt, more month than money, and not enough to buy my kids the things they really wanted and I wanted them to have. Yep, that was me. What about you? Can you identify with any of that?

When I became bold enough to proclaim I LOVE MONEY without the fear of someone quoting a scripture at me, my relationship with money started to GREATLY improve. One of my mentors told me that a long time ago he learned, Money can't talk but it does have ears and if you will call it, it will come. So, I started calling and it started coming. I figured there is nothing wrong with loving money. Just like there is nothing wrong with loving nature, clothes, or books. Money is an inanimate object that is neither good nor bad. I figured I am a good person, so I will do good things with my money. Maybe bad people do bad things with their money but I have nothing to do with that. That's not me. I doubt if that is you either. When you love something, it wants to be with you. When you don't like someone or something, there is a distance there. Therefore, I decided to love money because I believe in having lots of it around me. Always remember this about money. Money is a tool. You use IT and not people.

So how is your relationship with money? Let me speak about some great things regarding you and money. *You have a great relationship with money. Money is the servant and you are its master. Money comes when you call it. You are a money magnet. You like money and money likes you. It flows to you in large amounts. You make no excuses for having lots of money. You know how to handle it, give it, and use it wisely. When you give it out, it comes back to you at least ten fold. No matter what your relationship in the past has been with money, today is a new day. You have turned over a new money leaf. You feel worthy and deserving of lots and lots of money, and you always get what you deserve.*

"Ask and it shall be given. Pressed down, shaken together, and running over." Declare these money affirmations:

- I am financially free

- I am a 6 figure earner and on my way to 7 figures.

- I am a millionaire.

- My income is exploding.

- I am so happy and grateful now that money comes to me in increasing quantities through various sources on a continuous basis.

- There is no limit to the abundance I can receive.

- I am a money magnet.

- I love money and money loves me.

- Money flows to me easily, frequently, and in large amounts.

- I focus daily on my abundance.

- I am open and receptive to all people and ideas that help me achieve dramatic wealth.

- I operate in the overflow and always have an abundance of money in my bank account.

- I am financially responsible. I always earn more than I spend.

- I always have extra funds for unexpected opportunities.

- I own my home free and clear.

- It is easy for me to see myself in possession of the money I desire.

- I have a strong money consciousness.

- I use my money as a powerful force for good.

- Money is the servant and I am its master.

Your turn! Write here…

_____

_____

_____

_____

_____

_____

HEALTH AFFIRMATIONS

When I was a teenager, every Sunday we would go over my grandmother's house for dinner and get what my father teased was our weekly dose of sugar, salt, and fat. Grandma cared nothing about nutrition in her cooking, only about taste.

I feel blessed that my dad has given me a legacy of health. He has shown me the way in this area. If it weren't for him, I would probably have the same thoughts about health that most Americans have. Such as eat three meals a day from the 4 food groups, follow the governments food pyramid chart, acquire pains as you age, get prescriptions as you age because there is nothing wrong with that. Do the best you can but really you have to die of something anyway, so enjoy yourself and eat what you want even if it kills you.

Just like how most people have a bad relationship with money, most people also have a bad relationship with food. That's why more than 55% of the American population is overweight and over 30% are considered obese. We have grown up on happy meals, and fast food thinking the CRAZY thought that ordering a Diet Coke with it somehow made it okay. We enjoyed going over to Grandma's house every Sunday after church to get our dose of sugar, fat, and salt (this was my family Every Sunday going to my mother's mother's house). We ate fried chicken, greens cooked till they were dead with no nutrients left, and hydrogenated oil-filled potato salad. We thought that doing this each week, and sometimes several times during the week, was okay.

What about you? How is your health and your relationship with food? Does food control you or do you have great control over your food choices? Here is the great relationship with food and health that I see you having.

You look amazing and you feel amazing too. You are full of energy and vitality because you are intentional about your health. You minimize processed foods because you know they do not serve your body well. Instead, you make wise food choices that give life and energy to your cells.

Fresh vegetables and vegetable juices, unprocessed meats, plenty of pure cleansing water, and whole nuts and seeds are what you reach for first. When you put things in your body that's not the best for you, you know how to detoxify to remove it out. You have cultivated a lifestyle that keeps you in shape at your ideal weight and you are feeling great.

When you talk to yourself about your health, here is what you say:

- I am happy. I am healthy. I feel terrific!

- I have boundless amounts of energy.

- I am healthy and look 20 years younger than my age.

- I am sexy.

- I look fabulous.

- I make healthy and wise food choices.

- I am so happy and grateful. I do what I need to do to keep myself in excellent shape.

- I eat and drink only those things that are beneficial to my body.

- I feel great!

- I treat my body well and it responds with great health.

- I am strong and physically fit.

- My mind keeps my body in great physical shape.

- My sleep is always deep and replenishing.

- When I look in the mirror, I love what I see.

- The fit physical image I hold of myself in my mind is lived out in my reality.

- It is a priority for me to put exercise into my day.

- Good health comes naturally to me.

- I have a perfect memory.

- My immune system is strong and easily fights off what doesn't belong in my body.

- I pay a great deal of positive attention to my body.

- Everyday I take time to breathe deeply. I feel the connection between myself and all things.

- My body heals quickly and easily.

- I am the perfect weight for my height.

- I like who I am and I feel good about myself.

- I am beautiful inside and out.

Your turn! Write here…

_____

_____

_____

_____

_____

_____

SUCCESS AFFIRMATIONS

You know I can't remember when I made the decision that I was going to be successful. Maybe it was one certain day, or maybe it was programmed into me genetically and environmentally from my parents, I really don't know. When I started going after success, I started reading everything I could put my hands on that dealt with me being successful in the area of my choosing. I scoured the Internet, listened to self-development audios in my car (no radio) and searched for videos on YouTube daily even listening to them in my sleep. In all my reading and searching, I learned that there are certain habits that successful people all have. There are distinct ways that those who are successful think. Now mind you when I say successful I don't mean rich. Success can mean riches but it doesn't have to. I learned from Earl Nightingale that success is the progressive attainment of a worthy ideal. You are successful when you are accomplishing those things that are important to you and that could have very little to do with money. You may be accomplishing what you set out to do as a mom, a teacher, a coach, or an employee. If you are reaching your worthy goals, then you are successful. Remember that. I also know this. If you have not yet cultivated in you those ways of thinking and attributes that you need to have for success, they can be developed. That's great news isn't it? The affirmations in this book with help you to do that. If you are not persistent, you can become persistent. If you are not courageous, you can become courageous. You are going to need persistence, courage, faith, and desire to reach your goals. Here is why I believe success is destined to be yours.

Seek and you shall find. Ask and it shall be given. The desires in your heart are your prayers being offered up to God. He has already given you everything you need for the attainment of your goals. You are growing by leaps and bounds. When you get to the next level, you will continue growing from there too. Everyday you take time to focus on the personality traits, thinking habits, and actions that make the successful succeed and you are intentional about developing that in yourself. You've got what it takes, you can't be stopped, and you are moving on to victory. You are heading straight to the top. You encourage yourself daily with affirmations that help to develop in you, those things that make the great, great. Yes, that is you full of greatness that you show to the world.

Here is what you say to proclaim your greatness:

- I am determined.

- I am resolute.

- I am a winner.

- I am a champion.

- I am the best of the best.

- I am awesome.

- I am terrific.

- I take bold actions.

- I always get great results.

- I live my life by design.

- I live the life I want to live.

- Everything always goes my way.

- I dream big and I receive big.

- Whatever I put my mind to I accomplish.

- I move confidently in the direction of my dreams.

- Everything always goes my way.

- I love myself and I deserve to have it all.

- Every day in every way I'm getting better and better.

- I travel to relaxing luxurious destinations.

- I am full of great plans and ideas that I take action on and complete.

- I am organized and productive.

- I think purposefully.

- I attempt fearlessly.

- I accomplish masterfully.

- I use failure as a pathway to attainment.

- I easily attract the people who connect me with the resources I need.

- I have great habits that help me rise to great heights.

- My life is filled with good fortune.

- I always do my best in every situation.

- I am committed to the achievement of my goals.

- Every night I plan my work and every day I work my plan.

- My accomplishment is above average because I am above average.

- I am organized and efficient.

- My business is expanding, growing, and thriving.

- I do not fear problems; I solve them.

- I turn challenges into opportunities for me to grow.

- I think quality thoughts.

- My time is my life. I control how I utilize my time.

- I have a burning desire to be successful. I am success.

Your turn! Write here…

_____

_____

_____

_____

_____

_____

_____

 SPIRITUAL CONNECTION

AFFIRMATIONS

SPIRIT IS ME

It's not the part that you can see,

*But it's the **BIGGEST** part of me.*

Always was and always will be,

My Spirit is what's truly me.

No, it's not the part that your eyes can see,

*But it's the **GREATEST** part of me.*

One with God and God one with me,

My spirit is my deity.

It's never the part human eyes can see,

*But still the most **POWERFUL** part of me.*

Commanding life forth purposefully,

My Spirit is my creativity.

SPIRIT IS ME

by Iyabunmi A. Moore

Most people go looking outside of themselves to find the answers to their problems. The answers lie within. I believe that everything got started with Him and finds its purpose in Him. He is THE source. God is the SOURCE. The beginning. He is the all in all. He is in everything. He is everywhere equally present at the same time. He is in you. So why then when things are looking bad, challenges and obstacles are arising, things are looking grey and dismal, and we need answers, do we not turn to the God within us? We've been taught that it's wrong to think that we can solve our own problems. I'm here to tell you that the God power within you can solve all your problems. You have to acknowledge it and tap into it. That's where ALL the answers lie inside of you. And remember this, as within so without; as above, so below. Getting the right internal focus in line with your desires will produce the results you want externally. I believe in starting my day by connecting to the source that gets the day started. Whether you call it prayer or meditation, going into silence, you need to have that spiritual connection. While the body is important, we have to understand that the body is a reflection of the mind. Get your mind right and your body will fall in line. While on my search for answers to uncover the secrets of getting my desires, I really came to understand what nourishing your spirit means. This is what I learned. I am not my body. You are not your body. You live in your body but you are NOT your body. You moved into your body, and one day you will move out of it. You are not your name. You are called your name, your parents gave it to you, but you can change your name. So you are not your name. What we truly are is our Spirit.

For some reason that makes me smile. Spirit is what is really you. I was so inspired by the awareness of this a few years back that I wrote a poem about it. The poem you read at the beginning of this section was written by me. (Contact me for a framed autographed copy.) Read it again to grasp the true essence of who you really are. You are a spiritual being housed in a body having a human experience on this earth. So while your body is important, you can't be here without it, and your name may have great meaning, that is NOT the greatest part of you.

Grab hold of who you really are and focus on that part of you. Here are some affirmations to choose from to help you do that:

- I am fearless.

- I live by choice and not by chance.

- My faith is strong.

- I have strong mental powers.

- My thoughts and habits are of a positive nature.

- My words have healing powers. I use them to heal others and myself.

- Everyday I show my magnificence.

- I am excellence.

- I am filled with joy.

- I keep myself in a positive frame of mind

- I am an encourager. I am intentional about encouraging myself every day.

- My entire life is a miracle.

- I am aligned with my heart's desire.

- I have a bright warm positive outlook on life.

- I am the kind of person people like to be around.

- I am in the flow.

- I stay open to what the universe has to offer.

- I am connected to the energy of all creation.

- I am lifting my life to its highest calling.

- I create positivity in people around me.

- I always see the bright side of things.

- I have a winning personality.

- I am a great listener.

- I say YES to life and the universe says YES to me.

- I am a powerhouse. I am indestructible.The perfect partner is coming into my life.

- All my relationships are loving and harmonious.

- I have a pleasing, likable personality.

- Conditions serve me.

- My dreams manifest into reality before my eyes.

- I am at peace.

- I am in complete control of my thoughts.

- My mind works tirelessly to solve problems for me.

- My marriage is becoming stronger, deeper, and more loving each day.

- I am tapped into my God-Power. It helps me overcome all obstacles.

- God and I are one.

- I nourish my spirit daily. It's the most important part of me.

- The awareness of who I am is expanding.

- All creation is finished. What I desire already exists. It is mine NOW.

- I am tapped into my infinite power against which no earthly force is of the slightest significance.

- I possess the power of intervention.

- My inner world creates my outer world.

- I create positive thoughts from the power flowing to me.

- Those thoughts become my reality.

- I spend time each day in silence focusing on the thoughts and moods that I deliberately determine.

- I am the master of my fate.

- I am what I say I am.

- I am spiritually awake.

- God's love works through me now and forever.

- I am responsible for my own spiritual growth.

- I vibrate at a frequency that brings all good things to me.

- God's love flows through me, I am His, and He is mine.

- I am a divine expression of a loving God.

- All is well.

- I am the writer, director, and producer of the movie that is my life.

- I choose to accept only positive and Divine energies in and around my life.

- Each day I grow more spiritually aware.

- I am open and receptive to knock-my-socks off miracles in every area of my life.

- I am a miracle creator.

- I am enough.

- I am calm.

- I have great intuition.

- I am very perceptive and perceive the good in all things.

- My life is important.

- My life is on course with its purpose.

- I see my dreams fulfilled and live them out in my reality.

- I exude positive energy.

- When I walk into a room, people *feel* my positive energy

- When I walk into a room people feel my positive energy

- I am always divinely guided and protected.

- I am a spiritual being that is having a human experience.

- Spirit is transforming me. I am ever evolving.

- I am a shining light.

- My words have commanding power.

- I say to this mountain move and it is moved.

- I am guided every step of the way by Spirit who leads me toward what I must know and do.

- Unseen forces hasten to do my bidding.

- I AM.

Your turn! Write here…

_____

_____

_____

_____

_____

_____

 CLOSING

I hope you can be opened up to discovering and uncovering the magnificent soul that you are.

Whatever you want to be, you can be. Whatever attributes you want to develop, you can develop. It doesn't matter what your childhood was like, whether you grew up having or not having, if you were considered smart or not, or even what you have or haven't accomplished up till this point in your life. Whatever you want to be, you can be.

Before we end this book, just in case you are doubting if affirmations work, I want to explain to you on a scientific level why affirmations done correctly work. When you think a thought, a picture comes on the screen of your mind. We think in pictures. By impressing the picture upon your subconscious mind, the image will eventually manifest into its physical equivalent with you and through you. It's the subconscious part of our mind that executes what's impressed upon it and it is expressed through the body. Remember I told you to become emotionally involved in the FEELING of yourself already in possession of your declaration? When you get emotionally involved with your dream, you set up a vibration within every cell of your body that in turn sets up a magnetic force around you. This magnetic force begins attracting to it all the people, resources, and conditions that are in harmony with your vibration.

So there you have it. That's how it works in a nutshell. Now that you have the scientific background on how this works, you don't have to take what I say in blind faith, but you now can operate in FAITH WITH UNDERSTANDING.

You are more powerful than you know!

APPENDIX

For a video example of me engaging in my affirmation time, visit www.ImPowerMeNow.com

Get your FREE life changing mp3 tele seminar today, "Using the power of Affirmations to Change Your Life" valued at $97!

Visit: www.ImPowerMeNow.com

Connect with me on Facebook at
www.facebook.com/bunmi.moore